Kirby Muxloe Castle

LEICESTERSHIRE

SIR CHARLES PEERS   CBE, Litt D, MA, FBA
Past President of the Society of Antiquaries
Formerly Chief Inspector of Ancient Monuments

Kirby Muxloe Castle was begun in the 1480s by William, Lord Hastings, Lord Chamberlain of England and a prominent supporter of Edward IV. But he did not live to complete it: Edward IV died in April 1483, and before his son Edward's deposition on 25 June and the accession of Richard III next day, the latter had Lord Hastings summarily executed. Work at Kirby Muxloe soon came to an end.

The castle now stands much as Lord Hastings left it, as one of the most advanced and most fashionable fortified manor houses of its day. Visitors today can see the west tower, which was completed, and the gatehouse, while the foundations of the fortress and the earlier manor house which stood in its courtyard are laid out within the moated site. A tour of the castle begins on page 13.

ENGLISH HERITAGE · LONDON

Contents

Unless otherwise stated illustrations are copyright English Heritage and photographs were taken by the English Heritage Photographic Section

Published by English Heritage
23 Savile Row, London W1S 2ET
© Crown copyright 1957
Previously published by HMSO 1957
First published by English Heritage 1986, reprinted 1988, 1992, 1993, 2003
Printed in England by ABC Printers
Dd 6055228 C10 02/03 05650
ISBN 1 85074 123 9

History

The Hastings family

The buildings now remaining at Kirby Muxloe Castle were raised by William, Lord Hastings, shortly before his death in 1483. The connection of the Hastings family with Kirby began with the marriage of Sir Ralph Hastings to Margaret, daughter of Sir William Herle, who held the manor in the time of Edward I and II. Sir Ralph Hastings died in 1346, and his son Sir Ralph, born about 1334, inherited Kirby as the heir of Sir Robert Herle, son of Sir William.

In 1436 Sir Richard Hastings died possessed of property in Kirby, which Sir Leonard Hastings also held at his death in 1455. His son, Sir William Hastings, born about 1430, was the builder of Kirby Muxloe Castle.

William Hastings

William Hastings was a strong supporter of the Yorkist cause, and closely attached to Richard, Duke of York, father of Edward IV. On Edward's accession he was appointed Chamberlain of the Royal Household and Master of the Mint, and Chamberlain of North Wales (1461). In 1463 he became Receiver of the revenues of the Duchy of Cornwall, and in 1471 Lieutenant of Calais. He was summoned to Parliament in 1461 as Lord Hastings of Hastings, having shortly before this acquired the castle, barony, and honour of Hastings. In 1462 he was installed Knight of the Garter. He conducted various important embassies, and played a large part in the restoration of Edward to the throne after his temporary overthrow in 1470, commanding the third division at the decisive battle of Barnet in 1471.

Though in high favour with Edward throughout his reign, Hastings was not on good terms with the Queen, and at Edward's death in 1483 was considered to be more a partisan of Richard, Duke of Gloucester, than of the Queen Mother and her son Edward V. But the duke was evidently suspicious of him. At a council meeting held in the Tower of London on 14 June 1483 he denounced Hastings as a traitor, and had him taken out and beheaded on the spot. Shakespeare's version of the event in *Richard III* (Act 3, Scene 4) is well known, and in this connection it is interesting to note the tradition that Jane Shore lived for a time at Kirby. Hastings was buried in St George's Chapel, Windsor, in the north aisle of the choir, in a chapel which was made for him in his lifetime, doubtless as a mark of the King's friendship, and still exists. He was married to Katherine, daughter of Richard Neville, Earl of Salisbury, and widow of William Bonville, Lord Harington.

Lord Hastings was one of the foremost men of his day, and his reputation was as great abroad as at home. Philippe de Commines, the French chronicler, described him as a man of honour and prudence and of great authority with his master, and deservedly, upon account of the faithful service he had done him. It was de Commines who in 1471 secured his support for the Duke of Burgundy, by means of a 'pension' of 1200 florins. And when de Commines transferred his allegiance from the duke to Louis XI of France, he advised the King to enlist the sympathies of Hastings on his own side if it could be done. A 'pension' of 2000 crowns proved effective, but Hastings' acceptance of the bribe is a lesson in the art of preserving self-respect while in the pay of a foreign monarch. Louis XI sent his steward, Pierre Cleret, to London with the 2000 crowns in gold – his 'pensions' were always paid in this handsome manner – and with instructions to obtain a signed receipt for them, 'that hereafter it might appear upon record that the lord chamberlain, chancellor, admiral, master of the horse, and several other great lords of England, had been at the same time pensioners to the King of France.' But Lord Hastings, alone of all the 'pensioners', refused to give a receipt, and told the steward that the present proceeded from the French King's generosity, and not from any request of his. 'If you have a mind that I should receive it,' he said, 'you may put it into my sleeve, but neither letter nor acquaintance will you get from me: for it shall never be said of me, that the High Chamberlain of England was pensioner of the King of France, nor shall any receipt be ever produced in his chamber of accounts.' And to this he stood firm, in spite of Cleret's pathetic representations that Louis would certainly accuse him of embezzling the money if he returned without a receipt. Louis, however, quite appreciated the position, continued to pay the 'pension' regularly, and never asked for a receipt.

Lord Hastings' castles

Hastings was a man of great wealth, having been enriched by grants of forfeited Lancastrian estates, and in addition drew considerable revenues from his various state offices. By his marriage he acquired further lands and revenues, and the 'foreign pensions' already referred to added considerably to his resources. He was therefore well able to indulge his taste for fine buildings, and his work at Ashby de la Zouch and at Kirby gives a good idea of

his conceptions of architecture. Ashby is altogether on a larger and more ambitious scale than Kirby, but in both places the principle is the same: a domestic building of moderate defensive strength has been converted into a fortified house. (It appears from the accounts that the old house at Kirby had a gatehouse and drawbridge, base towers, and middle towers.) Ashby is the stronger of the two, and much more comparable to the purely military buildings of the twelfth and thirteenth centuries, but the essential difference is at once evident: in the early castles defence is the first object and domestic convenience secondary, but Ashby is first of all a great man's house.

Lord Hastings came into possession of

View from the south west, across the moat, of the west tower (foreground) and the rear of the gatehouse beyond. The gatehouse was left unfinished on Lord Hastings' execution in 1483

Ashby in 1461, its former owner having been James Butler, Earl of Ormonde, a Lancastrian who, after the battle of Towton that year, was beheaded at Newcastle. His estates were forfeited to the Crown, and Edward IV granted Ashby to Lord Hastings. A third Hastings estate in Leicestershire was Bagworth, and on 17 April 1474 Lord Hastings obtained a licence to fortify his three houses of Ashby, Bagworth and Kirby, and to make parks of 3000 acres at the first, and of 2000 acres at each of the others. If anything was done at Bagworth it was not carried far, for Leland, writing about 1540, says that he only saw there 'the Ruines of a Manor Place, like a Castelle building'. This might very aptly be applied to Kirby today; but at Bagworth the site is now marked by mounds only. Kirby, as we know from the building accounts, was not begun till 1480, and was left unfinished at Lord Hastings' death. The work at Ashby was well advanced before Kirby was begun, and Ashby remained the principal seat of the family. Its great tower, which, in England, is comparable to only Lord Cromwell's great tower at Tattershall, is even in its present mutilated state magnificent, and a lasting witness to the wealth and power of its builder.

A fourth building in the county, finer and more important than even Ashby, received very different treatment at Lord Hastings' hands. This was Belvoir Castle, granted to him in 1461 as forfeited Lancastrian property, having belonged to Thomas, Lord de Ros. Leland's account of the matter is as follows: 'Bellever Castelle', he says, 'was put in keeping to the Lord Hastinges, the which cumming thither apon a tyme to peruse the ground and lye in the Castel was sodenly repellid by Mr Harington a man of poure therabout and frende to the Lord Rose. Whereupon the Lord Hastinges cam thither another tyme with a strong poure, and apon a raging wylle spoilid the castelle, defacing the rofes and takying the leades of them, wherwith they wer al coverid. The Lord Hastinges caryed much of this leade to Ascheby de la Zouche, wher he much buildid. Then felle alle the castelle to ruine, and the tymbre of the rofes onkeverid rottid away and the soile betwene the waulles at the last grue ful of elders, and no habitation was there tyl that of late dayes the Erle of Rutland hath made it fairer than ever it was.' This was written about 1540. The old buildings, thus repaired, remained little altered until the beginning of the nineteenth century, when they were completely reconstructed, with the result that can be seen today.

Later history of Kirby Muxloe

The connection of the Hastings family with Kirby lasted till about 1630, when the manor came into the hands of Sir Robert Banaster. In 1911 the then owner, Major Richard Winstanley of Braunstone Hall, placed the building under the guardianship of the Commissioners of Works. The repair and clearing of the castle and its moat were begun in that year and finished in 1913.

The moat, which was partly silted up and partly filled with rubbish, was entirely cleared and its sluices repaired and put in working order. Very little was found during the clearing, beyond a few stones from the parapets, since anything that could be used as building material had been taken away from time to time. The tower and gatehouse were covered with ivy, and bushes and trees grew on the wall tops. Only the excellence of the mortar had kept the masonry from complete ruin. The chief damage to the brickwork of those parts of the castle which had survived was at the line of the water level in the moat. The action of the frost on the wet masonry had split away the facework to a depth of 1ft (30cm) and more, about 5ft (1.5m) in height of the wall being affected. The bases of the walls, having never been exposed to the air, were perfectly preserved for a height of 3ft (1m). The facework was repaired, to protect the core of the walls against further decay when the moat was again filled with water, with old bricks obtained in the area, which though not the same as the original bricks of the castle were sufficiently alike to harmonise with them. The west and south angles of the west tower were in a dangerous condition because much of the brickwork had fallen away, and were made good in similar brick. While the cores of the walls were as a rule sound, the pointing mortar in the joints was generally decayed, especially in the parapets and upper parts of the walls. The brick vaults were damp after long exposure to the weather, and had to be made waterproof by resetting their covering masonry.

In the course of clearing and levelling the area within the castle the foundations of the older manor house, of which all traces had been lost, were discovered, and were left exposed. They are easily distinguishable from the work of Lord Hastings.

History of the Building

Kirby Muxloe Castle lies on low ground and near a stream, in order to get an ample supply of water for the moat which surrounds it and forms its principal defence. It was planned as a rectangle 175ft (53m) from north west to south east by 245ft (75m) from north east to south west, with square towers at the four angles, a gatehouse in the middle of the north-west side, and towers of greater protection than the angle towers midway (except on the south east) in each of the other sides. The internal measurements of the court were about 100 by 160ft (30 by 50m). For reasons already given, the castle was left unfinished, but enough remains to show that the gatehouse and towers were to be of three storeys in height, joined to each other by two-storey ranges of buildings. These did not, like the towers, rise directly from the waters of the moat, but were set back, leaving rampart walks defended by low walls between them and the moat. The main entrance to the castle was through the gatehouse on the north-west side, but there seem to have been secondary gates on the south east and south west.

The history of the building can be described in detail, owing to the fortunate survival of the complete building accounts from 22 October 1480 (20 Edward IV) to 6 December 1484 (2 Richard III). The total expenditure for the four years was £1088 17s 6¾d, made up as follows: the first year, £330 3s; the second, £397 5s 8d; the third, £300 8s 6d; and the fourth, £61 0s 4d. The significant smallness of the last year's expenses, made by order of Lady Katherine Hastings after her husband's execution, needs no further comment.

The Controller or Clerk of the Works was Roger Bowlett, Bowlot, or Boulot, who acknowledges the receipt of £989 6s 8d given in instalments at various times at Birdnest, Kirby, Ashby, and Ley. At the end of the accounts is a summary in which the receipts are given as £944 18s 2d, and the expenses as £993 17s 6¾d, or exactly £95 less than the actual sum of the yearly totals.

When the work began, in October 1480, the site was already occupied by a moated house, approached through a gatehouse with a drawbridge. The moat was probably smaller than the present one, and in setting out the new building the old gatehouse and several other buildings were cleared away. The hall and the north wing, containing the principal living rooms, were, however, retained to form part of the new house, and their foundations may be seen today, within the lines of Lord Hastings' work.

In December 1480 the tiled roofs of the hall and various chambers were repaired, and throughout the winter stores of rough stone and of timber were collected for use in the new work. In February 1481 the old gatehouse was pulled down, and in March and April the debris of the destroyed buildings was removed, and timber for a new bridge prepared. The site of the old buildings is called the inner court, or the *placea*, the manor place, or simply *manerium*, the manor.

In May 1481 the work began in earnest, and the first mention of a master mason at 8d a day occurs. His name does not appear till some six weeks later, when he is called John Cowper. The leading freemason under him was Robert Steynforth, and it is worth noting that a considerable proportion of the men seems to have been

Welshmen, as were John and Hugh Powell, William Griffith, and Maurice Aprice. Carpenters then made a forge, using scaffolding poles and squaring timbers for the bridge and the postern (side entrance) over the new brook, and for what were perhaps a second bridge and postern 'made afresh towards the new park'. This was the park enclosed by licence of 1474. The moat was dug out and the lines of the new court laid down. A delightfully polygot entry, typical of the mixture of Latin, French, and English in which the accounts are made out, records the buying of 'iiij pecie meremii vocate le polles pro iiij Corneriis pro levelyng le erthe infra muros', that is, 'four pieces of timber called poles for the four corners for levelling the earth within the walls'. Freestone was quarried at Alton and brought to Kirby; the bricklayers were also at work, and hurdles, the medieval substitute for the modern scaffolding boards, were constructed.

In July the foundations for the walls of the courtyard were dug and rough stone foundations for the brick walls laid. A shed for the masons to work in was put up, and in August oak boards were prepared, from which templates of mouldings were to be cut for use by the masons. The sides of the moat were set out and finished, under the superintendence of one Davy Bell, and entries occur constantly of payments to men watching the moat at night lest a sudden rise in the brook should flood the moat before the banks were complete or the walls carried up above the intended water level. The laying out of the moat seems to have been finished by the middle of September, and the regular payments to 'dykers' cease from this time.

The work of pulling down the old buildings continued and straw, fern, and hurdles were provided for covering the new and unfinished walls and towers against the coming winter frosts. In October John Cowper, the master mason, went to Tattershall and back by order of Lord Hastings; Robert Steynforth had done the same thing on behalf of the master mason in June, doubtless in order to take notes of the treatment of the brick and stone masonry there. Through the winter of 1481–82 the work of demolition of old buildings went on, materials were collected and stored, and roads made.

In March 1482, the 'Basse tours' and 'mydultours' of the old house were being pulled down, and the building of new 'basse tours' began in April. The gatehouse was replaced by that which now exists, the rough masons working on its foundations in May and June. In April is an entry, 'circa facturam le murther holles de novo', 'for making the murder holes anew'. This cannot refer to the 'meurtrières'– holes through which missiles of many kinds could be hurled on the heads of attacking parties – in the gatehouse, as that building was then only just begun, and the probability is that it refers to the gunports. Floors and windows were put into some of the towers in May and June 1482, and by September and October the towers were nearly finished and covered in. In November 41cwt (2083kg) of lead was brought 'from the Abbey' – not further described – and added to 33cwt (1677kg) already at Kirby; John Smythson the plumber saw to the melting of it.

Building work went on without a break through the winter, which must have been a mild one, and in January 1483 the centering for the vault over the gatehouse was made. The new bakehouse and kitchen were then prepared for, their sites being levelled, and in February the gatehouse vault seems to have been finished and bricks were being laid over it. In March is an entry for 'botaillying in lee vootte', which perhaps means filling in the

The west turret of the gatehouse, showing the gunports and, to the left, the Hastings sleeve emblem in patterned brickwork

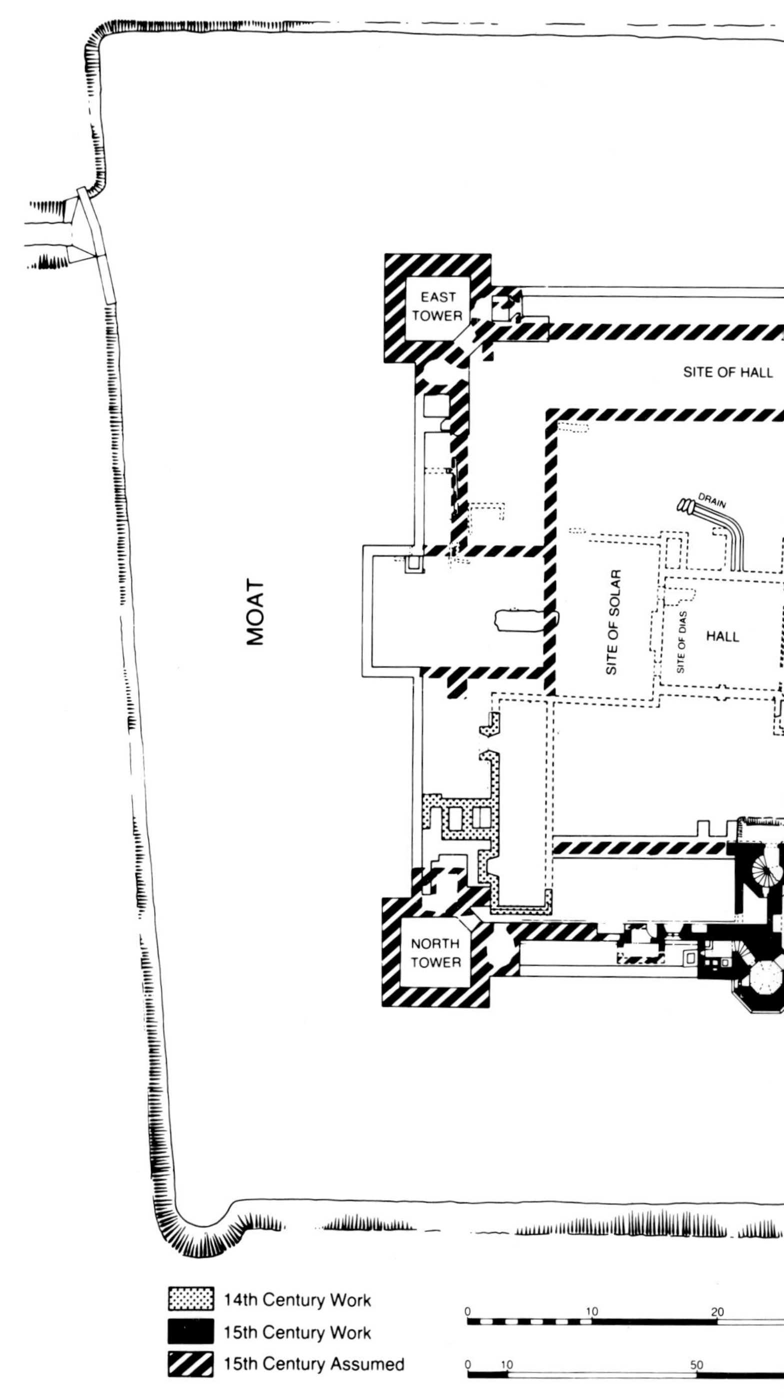
EAST
TOWER
SITE OF HALL
MOAT
DRAIN
SITE OF SOLAR
SITE OF DIAS
HALL
NORTH
TOWER
14th Century Work
15th Century Work
15th Century Assumed
0
10
20
0
10
50

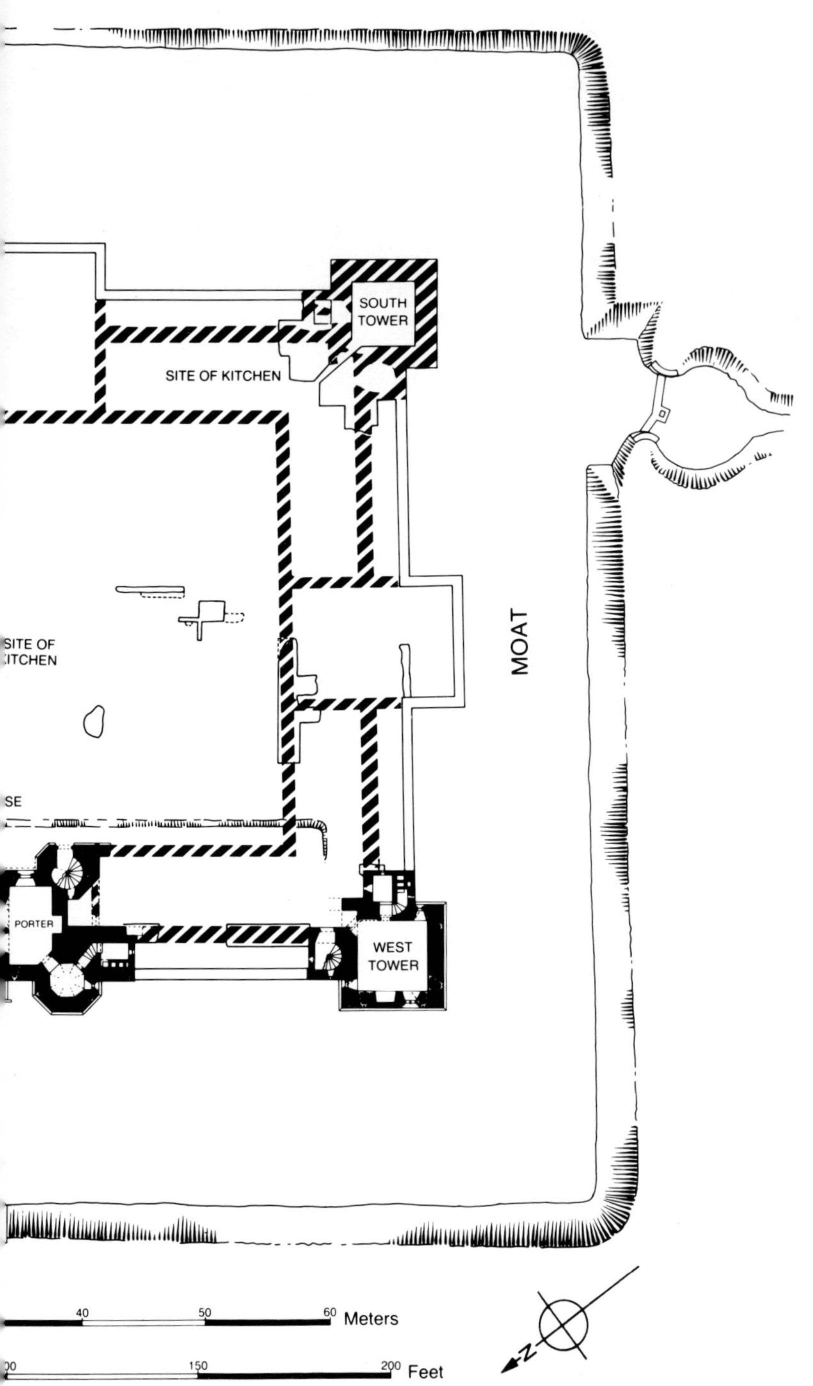
SOUTH
TOWER
SITE OF KITCHEN
SITE OF
KITCHEN
MOAT
PORTER
WEST
TOWER
SE
40
50
60 Meters
150
200 Feet
N

haunches of the vault, and preparations were being made for the bridge leading to the gatehouse.

Also in March 1483 the foundations of the new kitchen were laid, and at this date occurs an interesting account for brickmaking. Bricks seem to have been supplied by John Vaux or Fauxe, but the kiln in which they were burned was called John Eles Kiln. The burning of the bricks was under the charge of one Antony 'Docheman', who was paid 10d a week, as against 8d for ordinary men, and was clearly a foreigner, a Fleming probably. He is mentioned later on as Antony Yzebrond, and was then working as a bricklayer. He burned 100 000 bricks in the kiln in a week, using 78 loads of wood, that is to say brushwood and small stuff, and to make the newly cut green wood burn he added 'spyldyng', presumably dry twigs or the like. The site of the kiln, called the Breeke place, or Breke house, was evidently at no great distance from the castle, and affords one more proof, if proof were needed, that medieval bricks were commonly made in England and not imported. At the same time, the employment of a Fleming to superintend their making is worth noting.

In December 1481, and again in April 1483, it is recorded that worked stones from 'Swarston' Bridge (Swarkestone, Derbyshire) were brought for use at Kirby; evidently freestone was hard to get, and the temptation to despoil old buildings not to be resisted. The stones were used for the corbels or supports of the machicolations, and probably the slabs resting on them. In May lead pipes and gutters were being fixed and soldered.

Lord Hastings was beheaded on 14 June of this year, and his fall was reflected in the progress of Kirby. The bricklayers and masons stopped work at once, and from 23 June till 1 September accounts were rendered every three weeks instead of weekly. Practically nothing was done, but by September affairs had settled down, and the masons and bricklayers began again. John Lyle travelled between Ashby and Kirby 'to speak with the Council', no doubt a reference to Lord Hastings' own Council which continued to manage the affairs of the household and estate after his execution. The nature of Lyle's errand is not stated.

Work went on with roofing of towers and laying floors over the vault (of the gatehouse?) till November, when thatch was put on the towers and gatehouse for protection against the winter. The masons went on working through the winter, but the amount done is small in comparison with former years, and all through 1484 the work continued on this small scale, only £61 being spent in the whole year down to 6 December. Here the accounts end, and it is impossible to say whether anything more was done. The gatehouse was thatched in September 1484, and this being only a temporary protection shows that it was still unfinished at this date.

The accounts are full of interesting details, technical and topographical (see A Hamilton Thompson, 'The Building Accounts of Kirby Muxloe Castle, with Introduction and Notes', *Transactions of Leicestershire Archaeological Society*, 11 (1919–20), pp193–345). Freestone was nearly all quarried at Alton but rough stone for foundations came from a number of places, such as Bardon Hills, also called Barnhills and Baronhilles, Tiptree Hill, Ratby, Groby, Shawe, Steward Hey, and the Waste. Lime came from Barrow, sand from le Golet or Gullet, and lead from 'Wortesworthe Bolles'. Timber came from Loughborough Park, Bardon Park, Osbaston Wood, Sheepshed, Bradgate Park, Borough Spring, Crampes Hey, Colton Hey, Newbould and the 'new College of leye'.

Description and Tour

Aerofilms

Kirby Muxloe Castle from the air, showing its water defences and symmetrical plan. The foundations of the earlier manor house can be seen within the courtyard

The castle stands back from the road running through Kirby village, and is approached from the car park which leads directly to the bridge and gatehouse on the north-west front. The moat has been completely cleared to its original width and depth, and as it is cut in the stiff marl which underlies the surface soil, the slope of its banks and level of its bed is perfectly evident. Its greatest width from north east to south west is 300ft (91m), and from south east to north west, 360ft (110m); the width of the arms at water level varying from 45ft (14m) in the south-west arm to 70ft (21m) in the north east. While the north-west arm was being cleared the remains of an oak bridge were found, and may still be seen between the supports of the new bridge; it is reasonable to suppose that they belong to the bridge begun in 1483. At the inner end there was a drawbridge, the position of which, with the holes through which its chains passed, and the pit which underlies part of the gateway passage, are still to be seen. Low parapet walls rose from the side walls of the pit, where they projected into the moat beyond the front of the gatehouse.

13

Gatehouse

North-west face

A portcullis (defensive grille), the chase or groove of which may still be seen, defended the gateway passage at its outer end, and there were pairs of doors at both ends of the passage, opening inwards. The outer doors, which had a wicket or smaller door in the western leaf, have survived in a very ruinous state; they are of very plain workmanship for so prominent a position, and this may well be due to the failure of funds which followed Lord Hastings' execution.

The gatehouse is built of thin red bricks, varied with patterns in black: above the gateway are the builder's initials, W H; on the right turret the maunch or sleeve which formed the arms of Hastings, and above it a ship; on the left turret what seems to be the lower half of the figure of a man. All angles are of brick, stone being used only for doorways, windows, and string courses. The four-centred entrance arch is set in a square-headed stone-faced recess which runs up to the string course marking the first-floor level, and was designed to contain the drawbridge when raised. Above it is a square-headed niche with a panelled base and carved ornament in head and jambs (sides), which was intended to hold the arms of the builder. On either side of it are two-light windows with transoms (horizontal struts), lighting a large room over the gate.

The plan of the gatehouse is a rectangle with octagon turrets at the four corners, those towards the court containing newel (circular) stairs, while those towards the moat have small rooms on each floor, giving access to garderobes or latrines at the north and west of the gatehouse. The garderobe shafts do not discharge into the moat, but into vaulted chambers opening to the rampart walks.

North-west face of the gatehouse

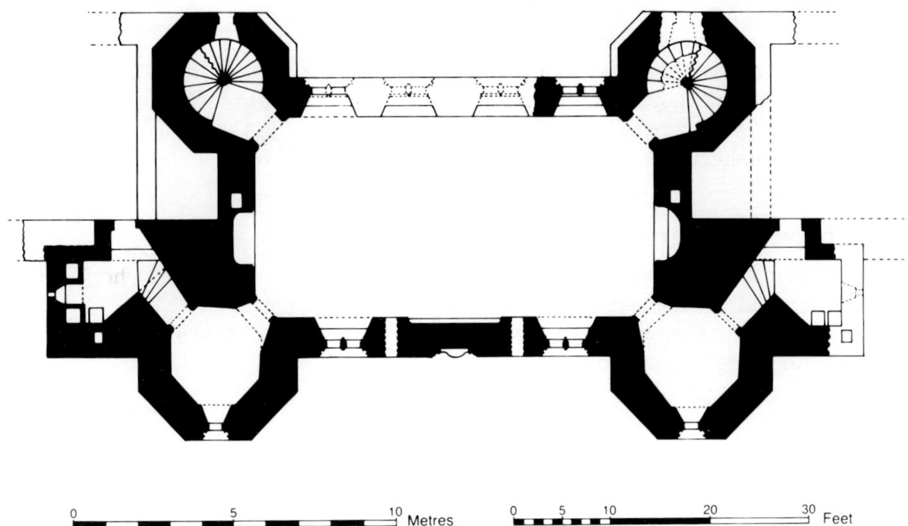

First floor of the gatehouse

Ground floor

All the ground-floor rooms of the gatehouse
are vaulted in brick, but the vault of the
gate passage has fallen. The rooms on either
side of the passage served as guardroom
and porter's lodge, and each contains a
large fireplace and a two-light window
towards the court; the porter's room has
also a window towards the passage. There
is no connection between these rooms and
the staircases, which are entered from the
courtyard, but doorways lead from them
to the ground-floor rooms in the north and
west turrets. These turrets have basements,
the earthen floors of which are below the
water level of the moat, but were originally
intended to be yet lower, by what must
have been a miscalculation of levels.

The embrasures and ports (openings in
the wall for firing through) for small cannon
are the most notable feature of the
gatehouse. There are two in each of the
ground-floor rooms of the turrets, one at
the north-west end of the guardroom and
porter's lodge respectively, and two more
in the basement of each turret, but these
are well below the water level of the moat
and could only have been used when the
moat was nearly dry. The gunports are
circular and have over them a narrow slit
10in (25cm) high for sighting; they are
widely splayed i.e. diagonally cut-away
inwards and their sills are at the same level
as the floor, so that the mounting of these
small guns must have been very slight.

First floor

The first floor of the gatehouse has one
large room with fireplaces at north east
and south west, and had four two-light
transomed windows towards the court and
two overlooking the moat. The floor is of
two layers of brick, laid flat on the crown
of the vaults below; this work can be dated
from the accounts to February 1483. The
portcullis and drawbridge were worked
from this room, but it was certainly
intended to be a living room also and was
perhaps divided into two by a wooden
partition. There was another storey above
it, but this no longer exists and was perhaps
never finished. It was presumably for the

front of the gatehouse that the stones from Swarkestone Bridge were being worked into machicolations in April 1483. The garderobe chamber in the north turret on the first-floor level has been made into a pigeon house in later times.

North-west range

The ranges of buildings running north east and south west from the gatehouse were designed with two storeys having embattled parapets towards the moat, but little of them exists beyond the broken wall-ends on the gatehouse, with remains of fireplaces, and the toothings or projecting bricks on the west tower. The condition of these latter suggests that the work came to an end before the ranges were finished.

West tower

The west tower is the best preserved part of the castle, and shows clear evidence of having been completely finished. It is in plan a square of 25ft (8m) projecting 6ft (2m) into the moat from the line of the revetment (retaining) wall, and has square turrets on the north east and south east, the former containing a newel stair and the latter the garderobes, the shafts of which discharge like those of the gatehouse into a chamber opening on the rampart walk.

The tower is of three storeys, with a splayed plinth at the ground-floor level, and weathered strings at the first and second floors; the two turrets rise one storey higher. The wall tops are embattled, with stone copings or protective coverings to the vents (indentations) and crests (raised parts), and the roofs were leaded and flat or of very low pitch. The general masonry details are like those of the gatehouse, but the patterns in black brick are simpler. Each room is lighted by a two-light window, and also by two single-light windows in the re-entering angles at north

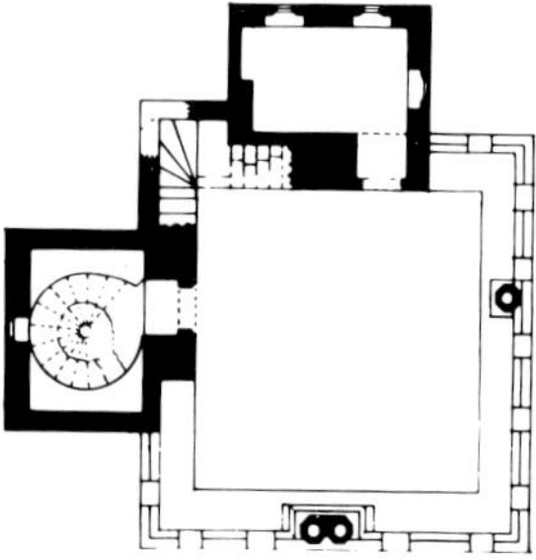

Roof Plan

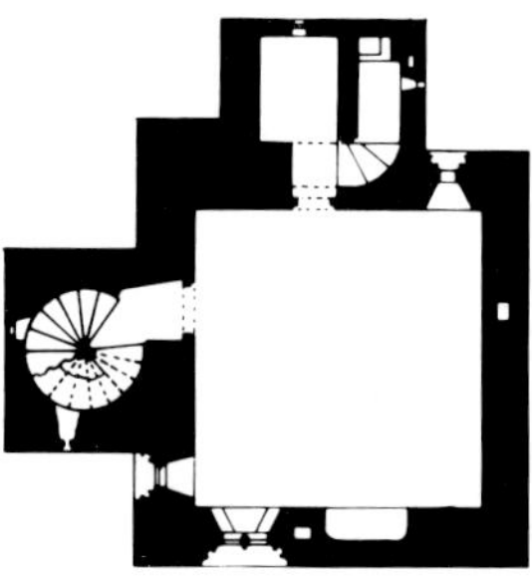

Second Floor

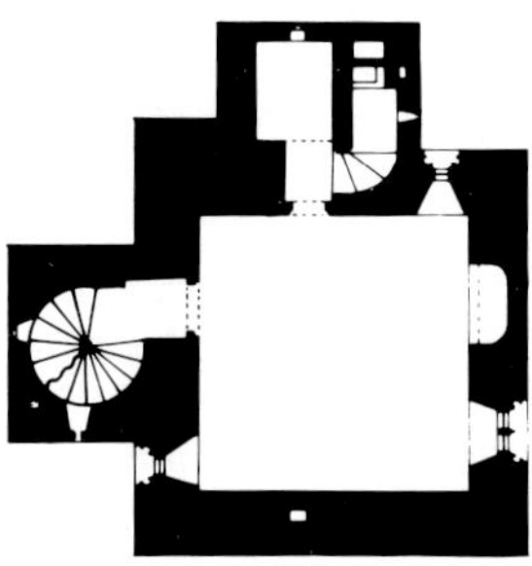

First Floor

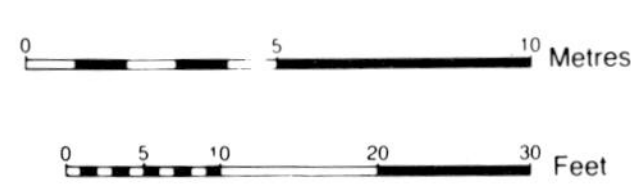

The west tower

The west tower viewed from the north west. The tower was the only part of the castle to be completed. Note the brick toothings for the north-west range which would have joined the tower to the gatehouse

and south. The fireplaces have plain arched brick heads, and two of the three octagonal brick chimney shafts remain.

The accommodation on each floor is the same, namely a large room with a small room off it, by which a garderobe is reached; the first floor of the gatehouse, as has been seen, is similarly arranged, though differently planned. Such sets of rooms were called lodgings, and were used for the household staff and for guests and their servants. The ground-floor room has six gunports, like those in the gatehouse, namely one on the north, two on the north west, two on the south west, and one on the south. There is also a gunport on the north-east side of the stair turret, commanding the rampart walk. These gunports for cannon are amongst the earliest examples in the country, and belong to a primitive stage of the science of gunnery. The diameter of the gunport is smallest at the wall face, instead of having a wide outer splay, and in consequence the gun only commands a limited field of fire.

Other work

With the exception of a short length of walling to the north east of the gatehouse, which shows the remains of a projecting bay and a fireplace next to it, none of the rest of Lord Hastings' work now stands higher than a few courses above the level of the ground floor. But it is clear that the plan of the north tower, and doubtless of the east and south towers also, was the same as that of the west tower. Little can be said of the 'middle' towers on each side, but the fact that the tower on the south-east front is pushed considerably to the south of the centre line suggests that it was intended to build a great hall between it and the east tower. The old hall would then have been taken down and the courtyard levelled. The kitchen, on this scheme, would have been at the south of the south-east range. It is quite possible, in view of the absence of foundations on the site of the older kitchen, that a new kitchen was at any rate begun, and is that referred to in the accounts for March 1483. It will be noted that the drain on the site of the old kitchen runs directly towards the garderobes in the east side of the south tower, just as the drain which starts from the south-east side of the old hall turns towards those of the north-west side of the east tower.

Of the earlier manor house, so little is left that its date must be a matter of conjecture; it may be mid-fourteenth century. The hall was of two bays, with the screens passage at the south-west end separating it from the service rooms and entered through porches. The lines of buttery and pantry (where liquor and provisions were kept and issued) and the passage to the kitchen are to be seen, but nothing of the kitchen itself is left. East of the hall, where the solar or great chamber should be, the foundations have been destroyed and there are traces of a cobbled path running south-eastwards across its site and as far as the moat; this has probably to do with later farm buildings, of which some rough foundations were found in the course of clearing the site. The north-east wing of the old house shows two projecting chimney breasts on the east side, with the pit of a garderobe or latrine between them; all the walls of this date are of stone, and it can here be seen how they were thickened with brickwork when incorporated in the later work of Lord Hastings.

An outer court is mentioned in the building accounts, and the ground to the west of the moat shows signs of having been laid out, although no foundations are now visible except those of a square dovecot. There is also a well to the north west, not far from the present road.

Brickwork

The details of the brickwork of the castle deserve careful study. The spiral vaults of the stairs, springing from the brick newels, are as skilful in construction as they are effective in appearance, and the domed vaults of the octagonal chambers in the gatehouse, with the brick corbels to carry the wooden centering on which the vaults were built, are well worth examining. Such detail as occurs on the brickwork was evidently the work of the 'brickhewers' mentioned in the accounts, and there is nothing to suggest that any bricks were shaped or moulded before burning.

Water supply

The arrangements for the supply of water to the moat are interesting. The brook and the little brook mentioned in the earliest entries in the accounts (October 1480) are doubtless much the same today. A masonry dam has been built across the brook just below the point where the little brook branches off to supply the moat. When the stream is low the water passes under the dam through a hollowed oak log, which could be blocked by a plug in a square hole at its upstream end, thus holding up a sufficient head of water for the moat. Across the mouth of the little brook are the remains of a screen of oak stanchions (supports) set diagonally, to prevent leaves, twigs, and rubbish being carried down towards the moat. Where this brook joins the moat is a second dam, with a sluice beneath it opening from a vertical brick shaft, which

can be blocked like the log at the upper dam by a wooden plug. When the shaft was cleared this plug was found still in position, and was a four-square block of wood tapering from 5 to 3in (127 to 76mm), covered with leather to make it fit tightly in the socket of the sluice. The outlet sluice of the moat at the south east was very ruinous when cleared, and a replacement sluice box has been set in the base of its masonry dam, to allow the moat to be emptied when necessary.

In the little brook, a few yards above its junction with the moat, there is an arrangement for diverting its water to the main stream, when there was a need to cut off the supply to the moat. This consists of a hollow log like that in the dam across the brook, through which the water can run into a stone drain leading south east to the brook. A sluice gate at the junction of the two brooks would have been a more obvious device, but the reason for the existing arrangment is that on the course of the little brook there was a fish pond – possibly more than one – the water of which it was not desirable to drain off except at rare intervals.

In the accounts references occur to a bridge and postern over the new brook, followed by the mention of a bridge and postern towards the new park, and it is not clear whether the two entries refer to two bridges or to one only. In any case there is no evidence of the existence of a third stream.

The site of the garden and orchard,often mentioned in the accounts, probably lay to the north and west of the castle, but this is only conjecture.

Glossary

Coping Protective covering to a wall, usually sloping and overhanging to carry off water

Corbel Projecting stone in a wall, used as a support for beams, etc

Garderobe Latrine

Gunport Opening in a wall through which a gun could be fired. Early examples were often circular with a vertical sighting slit above

Machicolation Opening in floor of projecting parapet, between supporting corbels, through which missiles can be dropped on the enemy. Often applied to the whole projecting structure

Marl The underlying rock in this area, a compacted silt

Newel stair Circular stair

Parapet Low, protective wall, usually at the edge of a roof

Plinth Projecting masonry at the base of a wall

Portcullis Movable iron or wooden grille, let down in vertical grooves (chases) in times of attack to block entrance passage

Postern Secondary gateway or side entrance

Revetment Wall built to support or hold back a mass of earth or water

Splay Diagonal cut-away surround of a window or doorway

String (course) Projecting horizontal band of stone running round a building

Transom Horizonal strut across a window